The First Aid Family

An Early Introduction to First Aid

Written by Annabel Wood

Illustrations by Brent James

www.alysbooks.com
Your Book | Our Mission

The First Aid Family
An Early Introduction to First Aid

Copyright © Annabel Wood
Illustration copyright © Brent James

Second Edition 2015
Published by Aly's Books

www.alysbooks.com
Your Book | Our Mission

Edited by Irrefutable Proof
www.irrefutable-proof.com

Designed by Fish Biscuit
fishbiscuitdesign.com.au

All rights reserved. No part of this book may be reproduced or transmitted in any form or by any means, electronic, mechanical, photocopying or otherwise without the prior permission of the publisher.

ISBN: 978 0 9941767 8 3

A Huge Thank You To:

My son Tyler, to whom this book is dedicated. Without him, I would not have been inspired to write this book. My daughter Hayley, who renewed my passion for helping mum's provide First Aid to their children. My husband Andrew for all his love, support and encouragement. All my friends and family who supported and encouraged me in this venture. To Renee McCormack who ensured the content remained in alignment with the audience for whom it was intended. To you all, I will be forever grateful.

Gary Glove

I am good to wear around yucky stuff

I protect you against germs

I like being used once then thrown away

You put me on your hands before you do anything

I am very handy

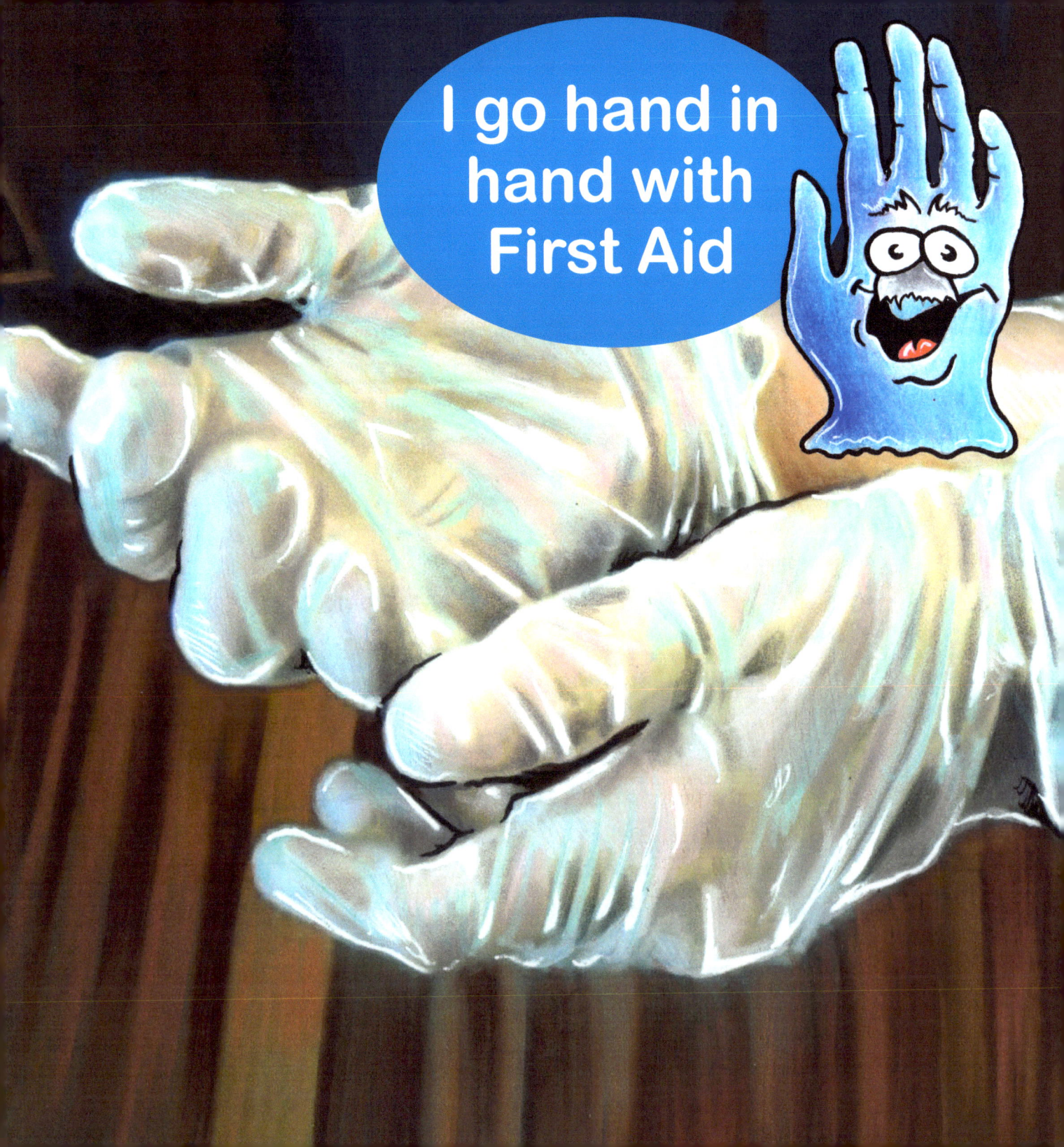

Chris Cool

I like to live in the freezer but I am happy in the fridge

I am very good at taking the hurt away

When my job is done I like to be washed gently and put straight back where I live

I feel very cold when I get out of the freezer – cover me in a cloth before letting me go to work

Benny Bandaid™

I am good at keeping your sores clean

I can help your skin to feel better

I can be found in different shapes and sizes

I like to be changed every day or when I get yucky

I like to cover small sores and scratches

TM

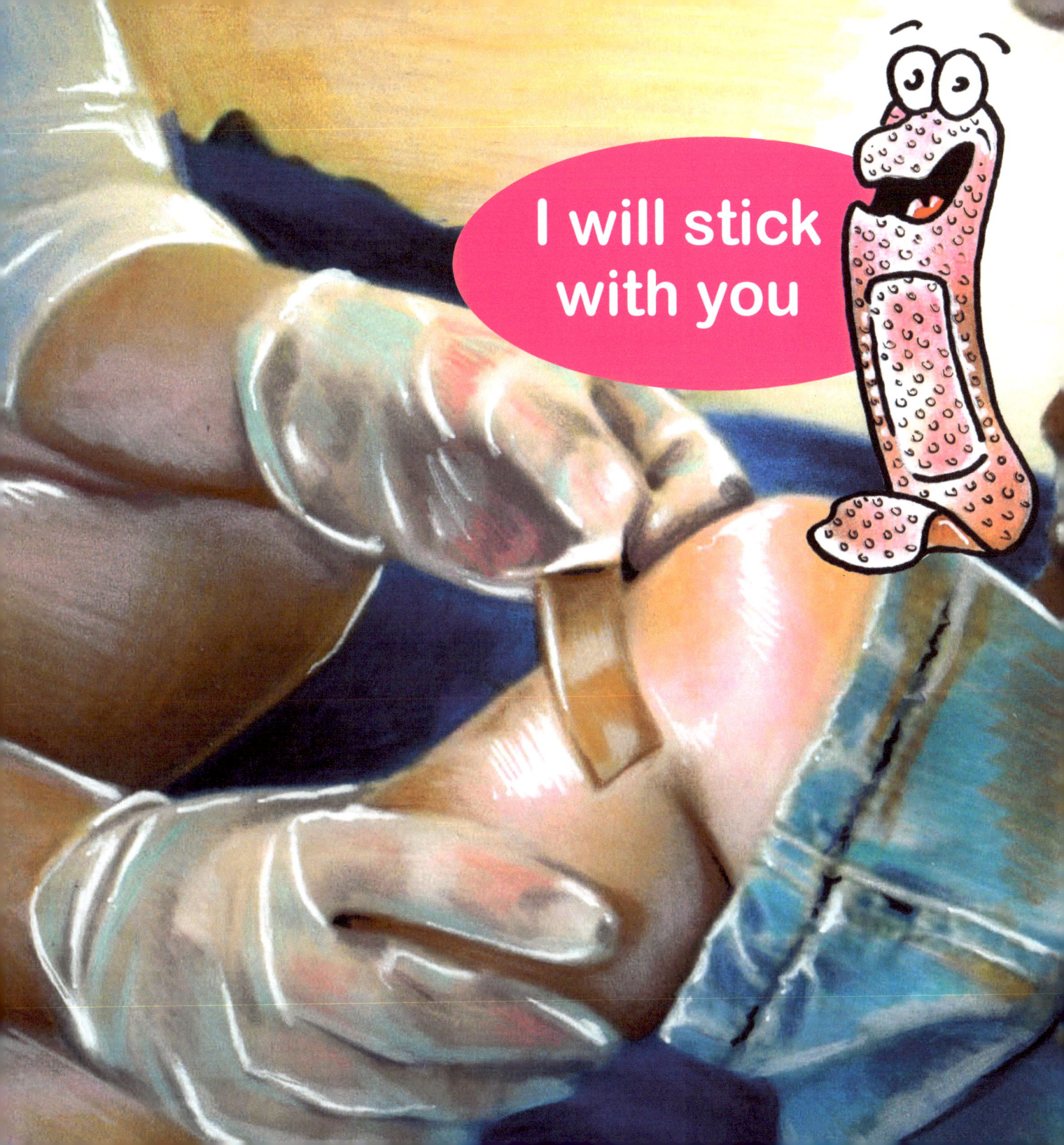

Daisy Dressing

I like the jobs that are too big for Benny Bandaid™

I love to cover up big sores

I can be found in different shapes and sizes

I like to be changed every day or when I get yucky

My best friend is Rowan Roller Bandage, and I also work well with Tina Tape and Timothy Triangle

Rowan Roller Bandage

I wrap around your sore arm or leg to make you feel better

I support my friends

I help bring the swelling down

I keep Daisy Dressing in place

I can be very strong when you are very sore

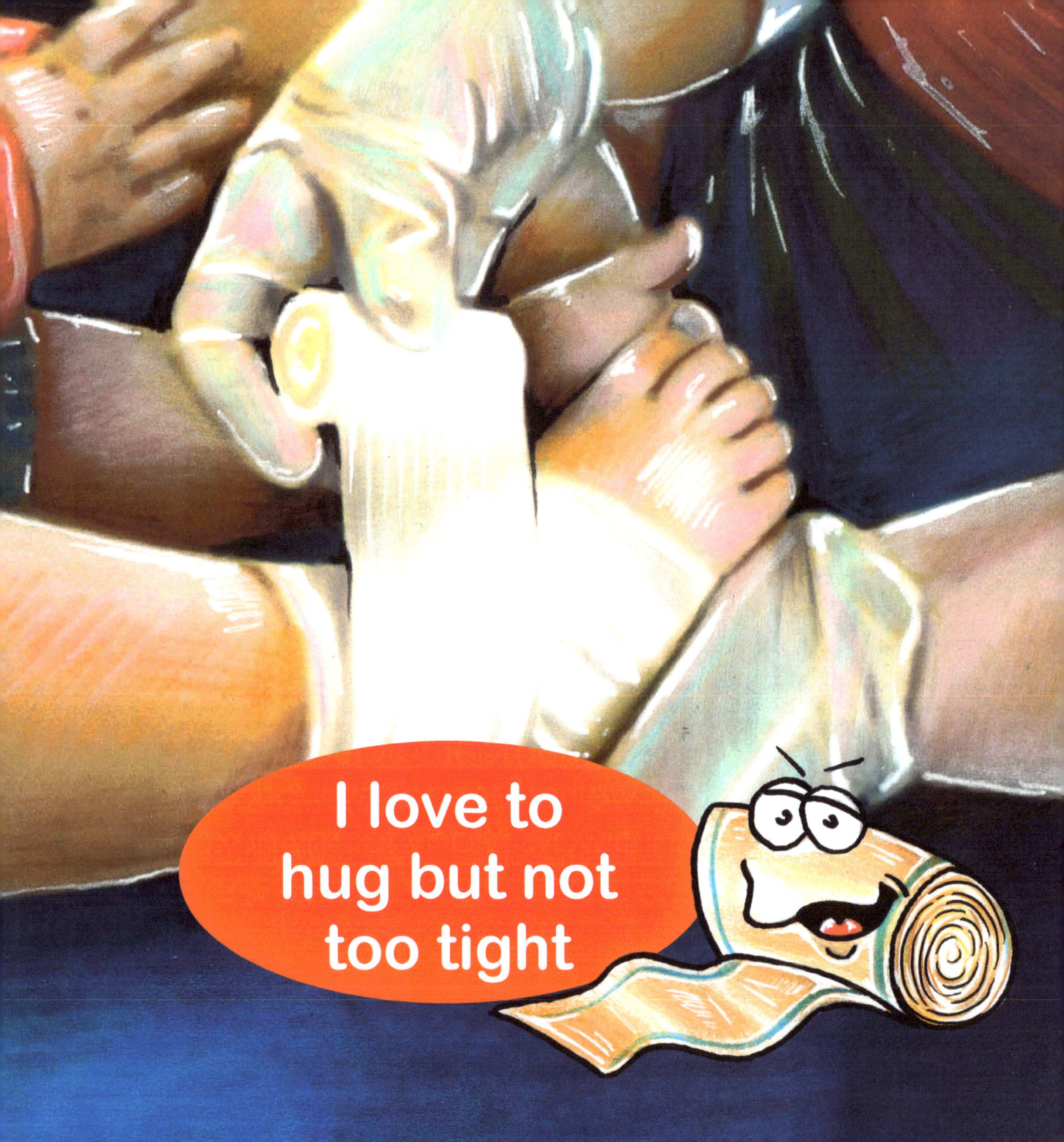

Skye Scissors

I cut Daisy Dressing into the right shape

I need to be used by big hands

Tina Tape is just the right length when I help out

Remember to clean me very well after I do my work so I am always ready for my next job

Timothy Triangle

My favourite job is to be a sling – I help support sore arms

I can be used as a few different things

I can be a sling, a dressing or a bandage

I am a very big and very clever triangle

I can also be folded up to a very small size

Fiona Forceps

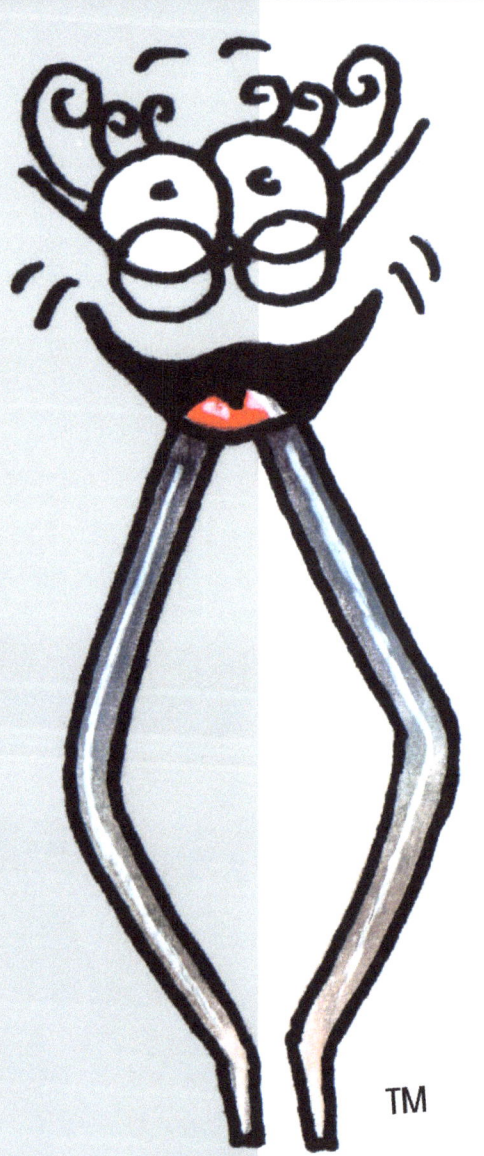

I like to pick up things that are too small for fingers to hold

I love to hold on to very small things

I am very picky

I like looking for bits of dirt, wood and other small things that might hide in a sore

TM

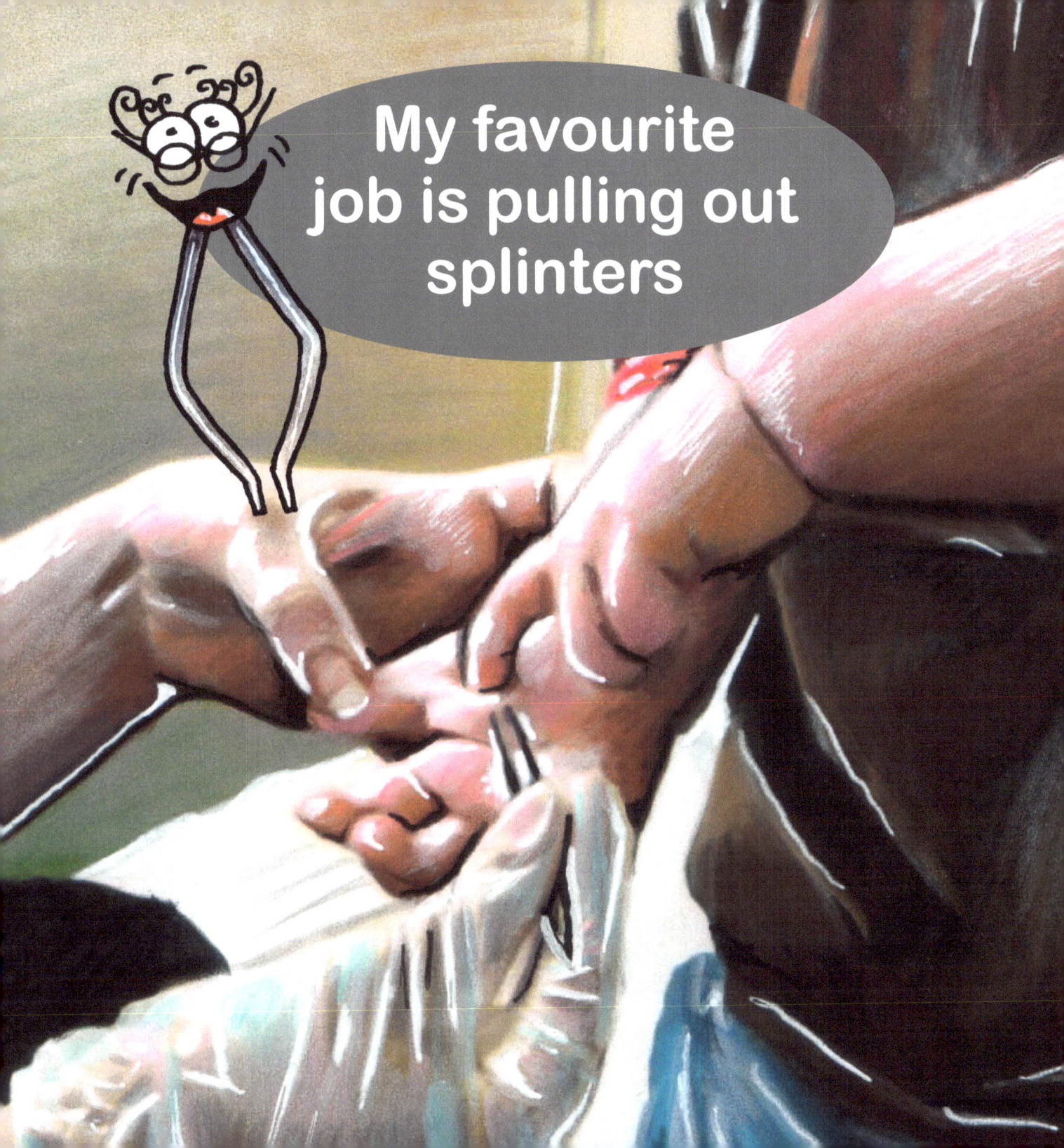

Tina Tape

I will stick around until the job is done

I make Daisy Dressing feel happy and secure

I love team work and never work alone

I will stick around while Rowan Roller Bandage and Daisy Dressing do their jobs

Phil Phone

Use me to call for HELP!

I help you call the Ambulance

Press the 0 on my tummy three times like this…

0   0   0

Remember to call 000 only if there is no grown up around to help you, or the grown up is not able to help you

Note: 000 is the emergency number in Australia only and will not work in other countries. If you are in another country, find out what your local emergency number is and write it in this book.

Fred First Aid Kit

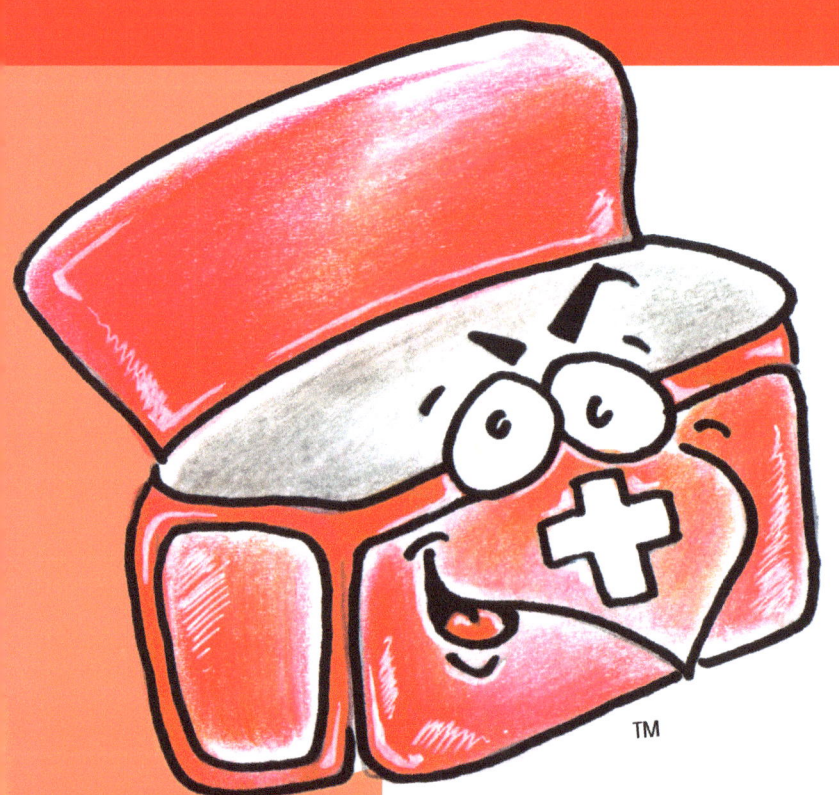

I am the First Aid Family's home

I keep the First Aid Family together

I keep the First Aid Family clean and dry

I protect the First Aid Family from pets, food and little fingers

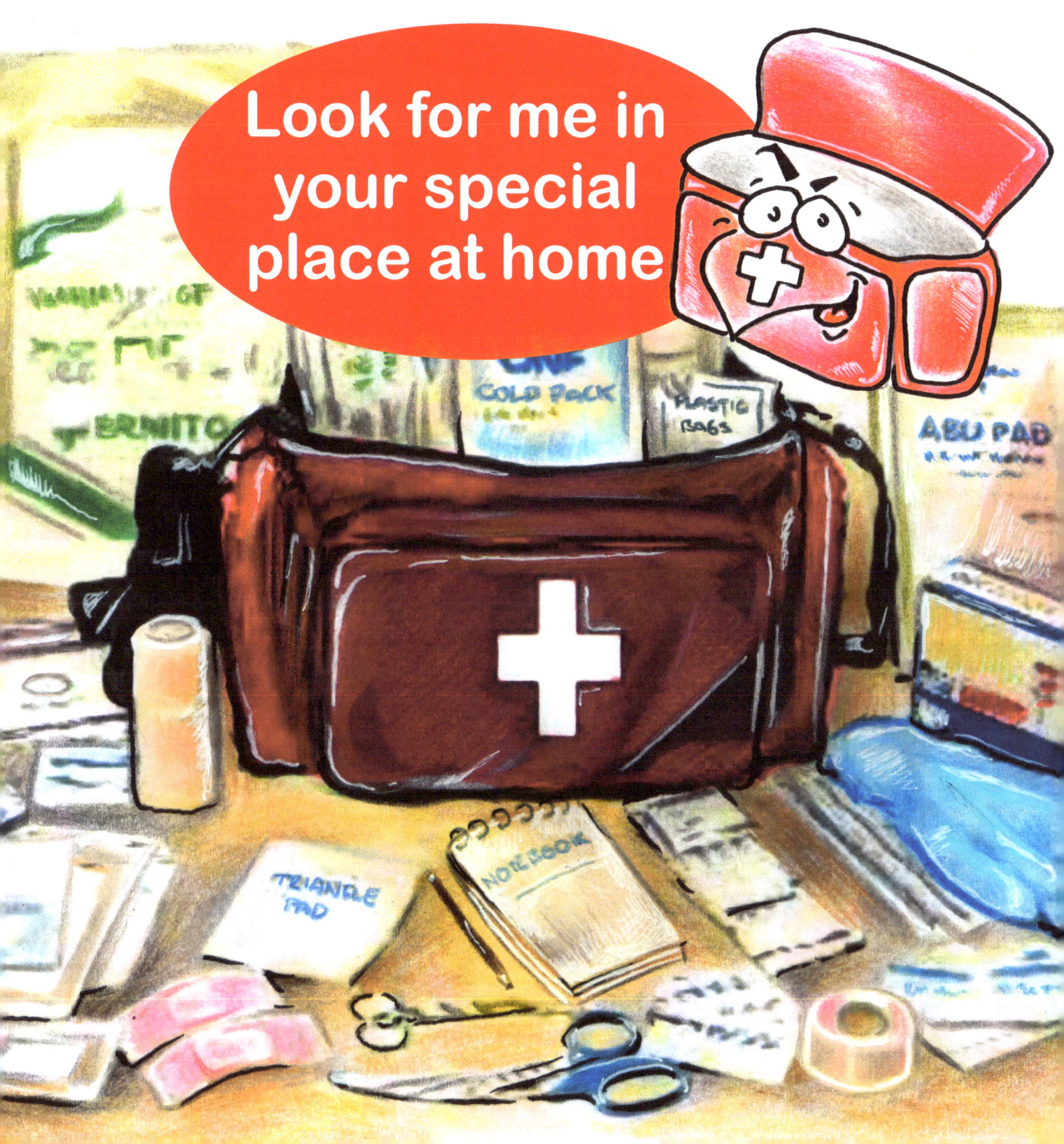

Remember these are only the very basic items found in a First Aid Kit.

As a child becomes older, it is important to introduce them to other items commonly found in larger First Aid kits. They are not mentioned in the book due to the unnecessary complication or confusion it may cause for younger children.

Discussion Questions

The discussion questions below are suggestions on where to start only. You may find alternative questions are more appropriate for your children. Also, the answers are a guide to help you to feed your children's hunger for more information. If you are asked a question that you are not sure how to answer, please contact the author for assistance.

Gary Glove

Q. When must you wear gloves?
A. Whenever you are providing First Aid, and especially when there is any blood or yucky stuff anywhere.

Q. What do gloves do?
A. Protect us against germs.

Q. How many times can you use your gloves?
A. Once. Then they must be thrown away.

Chris Cold Pack

Q. When would we use a cold pack?
A. If we hurt ourselves with a bump.

Q. What does a cold pack do?
A. It takes the hurt away by slowing down the blood inside that causes the hurting.

Q. What do we need to do before using a cold pack? Why?
A. Cover it with a cloth because ice can cause a burn if placed directly on the skin.

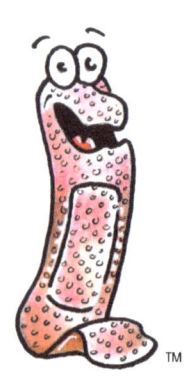

Benny Bandaid™

Q. When would you use a Band-Aid®?
A. If you have a small sore or scrape on the skin.

Q. What does a Band-Aid® do?
A. Helps your skin to feel better and keeps the germs out.

Q. How often should you change your Band-Aid®?
A. Every day, or more often if it looks yucky or starts falling off.

Daisy Dressing

Q. What is a dressing?
A. It is like a Band-Aid®, but bigger and not sticky anywhere.

Q. When would you use a dressing?
A. When the sore or scrape is too big for a Band-Aid®, or bleeding lots.

Q. How do you use a dressing?
A. After cleaning the skin, apply the dressing, keep it on the sore bit by using tape, a roller bandage or a triangular bandage, then change it every day or when it gets yucky.

Rowan Roller Bandage

Q. What do roller bandages love to do?
A. Wrap around your sore arm or leg like a hug.

Q. Why should we be careful when using a bandage?
A. If it is too tight, it might make it worse. Always ask a grown up to help put it on.

Q. When would we use a roller bandage?
A. To hold a dressing in place or to help the swelling to go away.

Skye Scissors

Q. Who can use scissors?
A. We all can, but only when there is a grown up helping.

Q. Why must we be very careful with scissors?
A. Scissors are sharp and can cause nasty cuts on your skin that hurt a lot.

Q. Why do we need scissors in a First Aid Kit?
A. To cut dressings, tape and bandages.

Timothy Triangular Bandage

Q. What can a triangular bandage be used for?
A. A sling, a bandage and a dressing.

Q. What can a triangular bandage help you with?
A. Broken arms, very sore arms or very sore shoulders.

Q. When would we use the triangular bandage as a dressing?
A. If the skin is bleeding and there is no clean dressing in the kit.

Fiona Forceps

Q. What are forceps?
A. Also known as 'tweezers'. Similar to chop sticks, they help you to pick things up.

Q. What kinds of things can forceps pick up?
A. Splinters, dirt, hair and other things too small to pick up with your fingers.

Q. What must you do after using forceps?
A. Wash them well then return them to the First Aid Kit.

Tina Tape

Q. What is tape?
A. It is like sticky tape, except it is specially made to be used for First Aid.

Q. What does tape do?
A. It helps the dressing to stay in place and stops the roller bandage from coming undone.

Q. How often can we use the same piece of tape?
A. Once only.

Phil Phone

Q. What is a medical emergency?

A. If there is a very big accident or a very, very sick person.

Q. In a medical emergency, what phone number would you use to call an ambulance?

A. 'Triple zero' or Zero Zero Zero (0 0 0).

Q. When would YOU call an ambulance?

A. If there is no grown up around to help you, or the grown up is not able to help you.

Q. When you call Zero Zero Zero, what will happen next?

A. You will be asked a series of questions so that the ambulance knows where to find you and how to help you:

"Police, Fire or Ambulance?" – say "ambulance", then you get to speak to the ambulance service.

"What is the address of the emergency?"

"What is the phone number you are calling from?"

"What is the problem, tell me exactly what happened?"

"Is he/she conscious?"

"Is he/she breathing?"

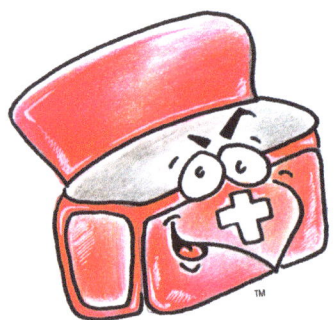

Fred First Aid Kit

Q. Where do the First Aid Family live?

A. (Fred), the First Aid Kit

Q. Where would you keep a First Aid Kit at home?

A. Somewhere clean, dry and easy to get to if needed quickly.

Q. When we have used an item from the First Aid Kit, what should we do then?

A. Tell a grown up so they can replace the item with a new one. That way it is always ready for little accidents.

My Emergency Contacts

My Address

Building Name

Unit Number   Street Number

Street Name

Nearest Cross Street

Suburb

Post Code

Home Phone:

Mobile Number:

Emergency

Police	**000**
Fire	**000**
Ambulance	**000**
Poisons Information Centre	**13 11 26**

Community

Health Direct Australia	1800 022 222
State Emergency Service	132 500
Crime Stoppers	1800 333 000
Police Assistance Line	13 14 44
RSPCA / WIRES	

Personal Contacts

Nearest Hospital:

Phone:

After Hours GP:

Phone:

Family Doctor:

Phone:

Plumber:

Phone:

Electrician:

Phone:

Other Important Contacts (eg. Neighbour)

Name:

Phone:

Name:

Phone:

Name:

Phone:

Note from the Author

My toddler, Tyler, bumped his head one day and I knew instinctively he'd need some simple First Aid comprising of a little quiet time and an icepack. As many parents of toddlers will know, the simple task of applying an icepack to an injury for more than fifteen seconds is a challenge to say the least! So how was I going to help Tyler? As a parent, a Registered Nurse and First Aider, I was well aware of the importance of applying an icepack, however my two-year-old had no understanding or concept of what I was trying to say or do. After several unsuccessful attempts to apply the icepack, together with my professional opinion that he would live another day, I discontinued my unproductive efforts. Needless to say, Tyler recovered quickly from this incident with no repercussions from my lack of ice application other than a small bruise on his head.

This event did start me wondering how I could teach Tyler to understand not only about the application of an icepack, but about other basic First Aid items too. I looked around for some printed guidance on how to teach young children about First Aid and was unable to find anything appropriate for him. Due to my passion for First Aid, education and primary health care, I embarked on the creation of this short book so that other parents and carers can teach their children that First Aid is not only non-threatening, it can also be interesting and fun!

Testimonials

Annabel Wood's 'The First Aid Family: An Early Introduction to First Aid' is a very clever and useful resource for teachers, children and parents. It is something that can be incorporated into everyday little accidents. It can also be referred to during safety discussions. We watch the children engage in play that imitates experiences that they have had at the doctor or at a hospital, and Annabel's book is an excellent tool that compliments children's interests and answers some of their questions. Annabel has adopted a simple but very effective approach to First Aid for children with her book that can be used in any environment.

Renee McCormack, Early Childhood Director

The 'First Aid Family' is a great teaching tool for any parent, teacher or carer of young children. As I read it to my 4- and 6-year-old sons, it created discussions around simple First Aid, from a simple graze to needing to call an ambulance. The Q&A section at the back of the book assisted me to answer my children's questions on which injuries would need which First Aid treatment.

The characterised illustrations with catchy names are perfect to gain and keep young children's interest whilst learning all about different injuries and how to help them feel better. It's amazing how just a little knowledge of First Aid can help to calm a child when they are injured.

As a Director of a Long Day Care Centre, I highly recommend this book as a resource for all Preschools, Child Care Centres and Primary Schools.

Penny, Teacher and Mother of two young children

Contact Details

Annabel Wood
Simply First Aid
PO Box 6642
Baulkham Hills
NSW 2153

www.simplyfirstaid.com.au

www.ingramcontent.com/pod-product-compliance
Lightning Source LLC
Chambersburg PA
CBHW041125300426
44113CB00002B/70